G000017909

Contents

Foreword & acknowledgements

Foreword

There can be very few motor sport enthusiasts who, if asked to name their favourite racing circuits in the UK, would not put Oulton Park at or very near the top of the list. Since it began its racing life over half a century ago, Oulton's challenging sweeps and curves and attractive parkland setting have made it a firm favourite with drivers, spectators, and – above all, perhaps – photographers.

Throughout the 1970s and beyond I was privileged to be a regular photographic contributor to *Autosport*, and also sometimes to *Motoring News*, as it was then known. In later years, I found myself writing the race reports in addition, so weekends could be very busy, as well as enjoyable. Working as a freelancer, my pictures were mine to keep once the magazines had finished with them, and, over the years, I built up a collection of thousands of negatives and colour transparencies which, after a decent period of storage, have been retrieved from the loft and arranged in some sort of order.

The first fruits of this reincarnation came in 2006 with Veloce's publication of *Motor Racing at Oulton Park in the 1960s*, to which this book is a companion volume. In it, I have followed very much the same approach as with the first volume. Tempting as it is simply to follow events chronologically, I have tried instead to highlight selected aspects of motor racing at Oulton Park in the 1970s as I saw them. For example, the welcome growth of interest in events for historic, ie post-war, racing cars and – to me, at least – the less satisfactory trend toward the now all-pervading 'one make' racing. With the loss of Oulton Park's non-championship Formula One races early in this decade, it has been interesting to look back on

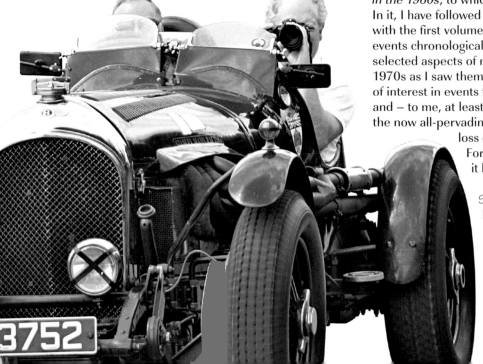

Still snapping after all these years. Donington 2007, and I'm working from the passenger seat of Richard Ford's record-breaking Bentley 3.8-litre which, in 1996, achieved a speed of 148mph at Millbrook. (Courtesy Phil Jones)

how well Formula 5000 filled the gap, for a time at least, until races could be devised for second-hand F1 cars which were becoming available in increasing numbers. And, of course, with 20-20 hindsight, it's been fun spotting the up-and-coming drivers and potential world champions who came to Oulton in their formative years to race in the junior formulae.

I have also followed my previous practice of including an eclectic selection of photographs from the period in the chapter Images of Oulton. Picture choice is inevitably a personal one, and, in making it, I have tried to pick out some photographs of the cars, events, personalities and views of Oulton Park itself which bring back treasured memories of motor racing there in the 1970s. They do for me, at least, and I hope for you, too.

Acknowledgements

In the 1970s, *Autosport* reported Britain's national motor sport in a proper degree of detail, and its contemporary race reports have made it the sine qua non of reference works for the sort of subject matter covered in this book. It has been my main source for confirmation or correction of distant memories.

Mike Kettlewell's 1978 publication marking Oulton Park's anniversary, *Oulton Park – 25 Years of Car and Motor Cycle Racing*, and both editions of his magnum opus, the *Motor Racing Directory*, published in 1979 and 1981, have continued to provide a wealth of useful and interesting information. The demise of non-championship F1 races at Oulton Park (and elsewhere) meant that I had cause to consult the detailed information on the subject contained in Chris Ellard's *The Forgotten Races* only briefly, but for which I am no less grateful. The original race programmes have proved most useful, as did the very small number of specialist web sites whose car and race data can be trusted. Among several people who have helped to fill gaps in my memory, the BRSCC's Tom Dooley helped put names to faces in several instances, as did VSCC member Mark Garfitt.

Peter McFadyen
Worcestershire, England

A memorable decade

It has been said that if you can remember the 'Swinging Sixties,' then you weren't there. By contrast, anyone who lived through the 1970s can hardly have forgotten this momentous period and the many events which took place during that time.

As that decade began, Pan Am introduced the Boeing 747 to its transatlantic air service; as it ended, the last Concorde had been built. Apollo 13 flew into trouble in April 1970; the Space Shuttle's first test flight took place a little over seven years later. VAT was introduced to Britain and our currency went decimal. It was the decade of the Munich Olympics, Watergate, and the 'cod wars' between Britain and Iceland. In the UK, we suffered the three day working week in 1973 and, in 1978-79, the 'Winter of Discontent.'

But possibly the darkest period – especially for motoring and motor sport – was in the winter of 1973-4 when the miners' strike and the actions of OPEC combined to bring on the energy crisis. Petrol rationing was on the cards and, for a time, it looked like we might even have seen our last motor race. Thankfully, matters weren't quite that bad. Rallying, predominantly a winter activity in the UK, was hit and, in America, the early season Daytona 24 hour race was cancelled, NASCAR races were shortened by 10 per cent, and qualifying at Indianapolis was cut from four days to two. By the time that spring arrived in the UK, however, things were looking much better and racing restarted almost as if nothing had happened.

But something had happened, of course. Thanks to OPEC, the price of a gallon of petrol in the UK rose from around 33 pence in 1970 to 73p by 1975, and was more than 98p by 1979: for comparison, by 2005 a gallon of unleaded fuel cost £3.96 (source: The AA Motoring Trust).

Motor racing, too, was changing fast, Formula 1 moving to confine itself to a dozen or so World Championship Grands Prix, still mostly in Europe, with the days of non-championship races such as Oulton Park's Gold Cup severely numbered. In the UK, the distinction between Club and National level motor sport was harder to define as more and more races became rounds of one season-long championship or another. The old order was definitely changing.

The early days of Oulton Park as a racing circuit are briefly described in Motor Racing at Oulton Park in the 1960s (Veloce Publishing, 2006). From its inception, Oulton Park was owned and managed by Cheshire Car Circuits Ltd under the leadership of Rex Foster. In 1964 the company became a subsidiary of Brands Hatch-based Motor Circuit Developments, MCD, one of the companies owned by Grovewood Securities which, shortly afterward, acquired the freehold of Oulton Park. John Webb, MCD's Managing Director and one time press officer at Brands Hatch, played an active and major role in British motor racing during the 1960s and 1970s, and MCD's rule was to continue well into the following decade.

The last occasion on which a driver who had already won the World Championship was to compete in a major race at Oulton Park was the 1972 Gold Cup race, when Denny Hulme also became the last driver to win there in a contemporary F1 car (Emerson Fittipaldi, who finished second in that race, would not become World Champion until the end of the season). Without Formula 1, and with no more opportunities for spectators to see some of the world's best known drivers and cars in action on the challenging Cheshire circuit, it was understandable that some began to express doubt about Oulton Park's long term future as a major race venue. Fortunately,

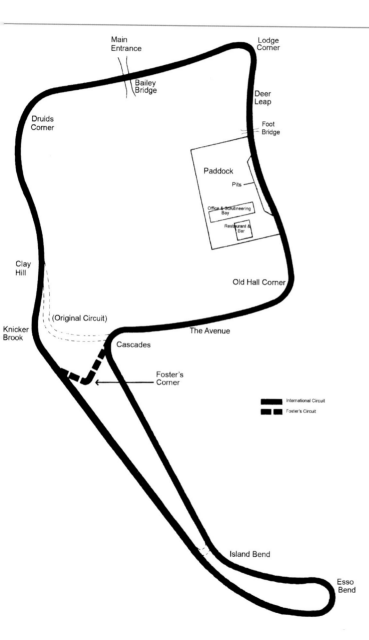

Main Entrance
Lodge Corner
Bailey Bridge
Deer Leap
Druids Corner
Foot Bridge
Paddock
Pits
Office & Scrutineering Bay
Restaurant & Bar
Old Hall Corner
Clay Hill
(Original Circuit)
The Avenue
Knicker Brook
Cascades
Foster's Corner

■■■ International Circuit
■ ■ ■ Foster's Circuit

Island Bend
Esso Bend

The new 1.654 mile Foster's Circuit came into use for the first time with the Shellsport F5000 Championship meeting at Easter 1975. That, of course, was the occasion when heavy snow prevented practice on the Thursday preceding the Good Friday racing. By the following day, however, the snow was clearing fast and the meeting went ahead.

the answer was to be found in the rapid growth in popularity and stature of national racing. With more and more competitors racing in an ever-growing number of championships, UK motor racing rose to fill the void, helped on by Formula 5000 and, later, a national Formula 1 championship, both, incidentally, owing their existence in large measure to John Webb.

Freed from the demands of the major international race formulae for a circuit to be over a certain minimum length, Oulton Park's management made the bold decision to shorten the circuit by building a link road from Cascades to rejoin the full circuit at the end of the straight just before Knicker Brook. The result, ironically, was a circuit very similar in layout to that of the original Oulton Park when it had begun life 22 years earlier.

The new, shorter version of Oulton Park was far from universally popular. Reporting the opening meeting, *Autosport* referred to "the abbreviation of what used to be Britain's best circuit," and that was mild compared with some of the comments! The authorities, naturally enough, were keen to point to the other side of the coin. Unlike the now disused Island and Esso bends, they said, the new corner was in full view of the public and, being a very tight bend, they were anticipating "... a great deal of sideways motoring to negotiate it quickly." They forecast that it would become "... the new focal point of attention at Oulton." As it turned out, it wasn't long before the exit of

The 'honour' of leading the first racing lap through the new – and, as yet, unnamed – tight right-hander fell to Andy Rouse, who led the National Touring Car race from start to finish in the Team Piranha Triumph Dolomite.

Foster's, as it was to become known, had to be widened to relieve some of the tightness and enable more cars to survive a race without damage.

What the circuit alteration did undoubtedly bring about was shorter lap times (which, in turn, meant that spectators all around Oulton Park saw the cars more often) and, for competitors, more ten-lap races could be packed into a day's programme. For photographers, it has to be said, Foster's did provide some new opportunities and plenty of action, although only at the expense of one of the best backdrops in British motor racing: the approach to Esso with the lake in the background.

In the fifties and sixties, races were generally for 'sports cars,' 'racing cars' or for 'saloon cars,' perhaps divided within an event into classes that were usually decided by engine capacity. As more cars began competing, these broad classifications were themselves subdivided. Thus, by the seventies, we had, for example, 'Production Saloons' separated from the more modified

Another factor which must have been of some benefit to the circuit owners – although one which I never heard mentioned – was that, with over 1.1 fewer miles of track to maintain, cost savings must have been considerable. As the picture of Tony Brise's F3 March negotiating Knicker Brook in September 1973 clearly shows, the track surface required constant attention if it was to be maintained in a condition that was safe and fit for the rapidly increasing corner speeds of the new generations of winged and slick-shod racing cars.

'Special Saloons.' We became used to 'ModSports' being different from 'ProdSports,' and all were further split into several classes according to engine size and, in some cases, the car's list price.

Eventually, even this arrangement was not enough and races and championships were devised which catered for just a single make or model. One-make racing began to proliferate during the 1970s and resulted in races being devised for, among others, Ford Escort Mexicos, Sunbeams, Renault 5s and Minis in several different sizes, all of which raced among themselves but not with each other. Racing was usually wheel to wheel so it could be entertaining to watch – but what had happened to variety?

One answer to that cry was to be found in another form of racing – historic motor sport – which is

massively popular today but was just getting off the ground in the 1970s. Thanks in large measure to Bill Allen and Nigel Moores, and enthusiastic backing by Anthony Bamford and his company, the JCB-Speed Merchants Championship for historic cars, primarily sports cars, revived a host of wonderful 1950s and 60s cars to race together once again on the circuits of Britain. At Oulton Park, these races usually supported the major events of the year, with entry lists for the historic race, frankly, sometimes putting the main event to shame! The Lancashire & Cheshire Car Club's race meeting in August each year came to feature historic and modern races in equal measure, and were all the better for it.

Meanwhile, let's not forget the Vintage Sports Car Club's annual Seaman Trophies meeting, a highlight in the calendar of both the VSCC and Oulton Park. The

VSCC first brought its unique style of racing for pre-war cars to Oulton Park in 1956, later embracing pre-1961 front engined racing (but not sports) cars in the programme of events. The VSCC's summer visits to Cheshire certainly brought variety aplenty, as did the efforts of the Historic Sports Car Club which formulated many of the rules for historic motor racing. The HSCC ran its championships at events organised by other clubs until, late in the seventies, it took to running its own meetings which, as this book is written, include the Oulton Park Gold Cup meeting,

Tony Walker in the beautiful 3-litre Maserati 300S, rounding Esso Bend during the L&CCC meeting in August 1973. The Maserati was typical of the cars given a new lease of life with the introduction of events for historic sports cars.

now one of the Club's major events of the year. This three-day festival, held over the August bank holiday weekend, is ample testimony to the growth and success of historic racing which, back in the seventies, was only just beginning.

The main event

Since 1954, the circuit's first full year of operation, the Oulton Park Gold Cup has always been the highlight and main event of the Cheshire venue's motor racing season. The list of winners is certainly impressive, headed by Stirling Moss who won on five occasions and was given the original Gold Cup to keep! Jack Brabham scored four wins, John Surtees three, whilst Jim Clark and Roy Salvadori each triumphed twice. Single Gold Cup winners include Jackie Stewart, Jacky Ickx, Denny Hulme, and Peter Gethin. Usually run as a non-championship Formula One race, sometimes Formula Two, the event gave Oulton Park spectators a chance to see some of the world's top drivers racing the latest works Grand Prix cars. While the Gold Cup was traditionally run in autumn, the Easter weekend came to be another major date on the Oulton Park calendar, the Good Friday car meeting often providing an early-season opportunity for British-based Grand Prix teams to try out their latest designs under race conditions.

As more and more countries hosted Grands Prix of their own, Formula One moved inexorably toward being a World Championship-only affair. Non-championship races began to fall from favour, and entry lists were opened up to other types of car in an effort to fill the grids. At the start of the decade, the 1970 Gold Cup fielded only six F1 cars, albeit four of them in the hands of past or future world champions – Graham Hill, John Surtees, Jackie Stewart, and Jochen Rindt. The rest of the entry was made up of Formula 5000 cars, the 5-litre, V-8-engined single seaters well able to mix it with the 3-litre purebred Grand Prix cars.

In April 1971, the Rothmans/*Daily Express* International Trophy on Good Friday was restricted to F1 cars. Twelve entries were reduced to just eleven starters when local favourite, Cyd Williams, suffered a massive accident during untimed practice the day before the race. Pedro Rodriguez emerged the winner in his V-12, Yardley-sponsored BRM P160. The Guards Gold Cup in August attracted works F1 entries from BRM, Surtees, and Williams, plus four privateers along with twelve F5000 cars from the Rothmans Championship, John Surtees repeating his win of the previous year.

For 1972, the Gold Cup was brought forward to the bank holiday Monday in May in the hope of attracting more entries, but a competing attraction, Crystal Palace's last F2 race before the London circuit closed, caught the attention of several drivers who might otherwise have gone to Oulton. It fell to ten of the cars that had competed a few hours earlier in the Rothmans European F5000 Championship race to come to the rescue and join the select band of eight F1 cars on the grid. Denny Hulme's McLaren won the race from Emerson Fittipaldi's Lotus 72D, with another Oulton favourite, Brian Redman (Chevron B24), heading the F5000s home in fourth place. Although Hulme had won the Tourist Trophy sports car race at Oulton no fewer than three times in the past, it was his first Gold Cup victory; as it turned out, he was the last driver ever to win at Oulton Park in a contemporary F1 car.

On the bright side, Formula 5000 was at its peak in 1973, and the sixth round of that year's Rothmans European F5000 Championship, held at Oulton Park in May, produced the sixth different winner, Teddy Pilette. Not only was the series competitive but the F5000 cars were fast – Peter Gethin lapped 0.4s inside Hulme's F1 and outright circuit record during qualifying for the Gold Cup in September – and they were certainly spectacular to watch. Above all, they turned out in decent numbers, with eighteen starters in the Gold Cup race.

With various rule changes, principally to allow

John Surtees (Surtees-Ford Cosworth DFV TS7) won the two-part 1970 Gold Cup race from Jochen Rindt's Lotus 72.
Here, he passes the pits during the very wet practice period on the day before the race.

One of the most experienced drivers in F5000, former McLaren and BRM Grand Prix driver who memorably won the 1971 Italian GP, Peter Gethin, was series champion in 1969 and 1970. Arriving in the Oulton Park paddock for the Good Friday meeting and checking the latest publicity, he later qualified alongside his team-mate, Teddy Pilette, on the front row. Unfortunately, a collision between the two was to put him out of the race.

smaller, more highly developed engines to compete alongside the push-rod V8s, F5000 remained centre stage at Oulton for two more years before circuit owner MCD* moved to open up the series to include F1, F2 and Formula Atlantic cars as well as F5000s. The category was known as Group 8, although the championship itself continued as the Shellsport F5000 Championship. Spectators were obviously keen, an estimated 25,000 of them turning out for the first race on Good Friday, 1976. Damien Magee's ex-Thursday's nightclub-sponsored March, with 3.4-litre Cosworth engine, won the race for which there were 27 entries and 22 starters. Several of the F1 cars proved highly competitive, prompting Ian Titchmarsh to write in *Autosport* that "... a Formula 1 car will win an F5000 race soon," an interesting reversal of roles compared with earlier years of mixed fields! But how right he was – Guy Edwards' Brabham BT42/44 won the very next Oulton Park race, the Gold Cup in September, ahead of Brian Henton's F2 Boxer.

Although mostly Cosworth DFV-engined 'kit cars,' the F1s were back in charge, Tony Trimmer taking the 1977 championship in a Surtees TS19, and Derek Bell – making a welcome return to Oulton Park – winning the Gold Cup in a Penske PC3. By the following year, the F5000s were gone and the Aurora AFX F1 Championship was the main focus of interest. It got away to an inauspicious start with the 1978 Gold Cup race in March, only twelve of the eighteen entries making the start, four of them F2 cars for which there was a separate championship class. Trimmer, this time at the wheel of the last McLaren M23 built, was again victorious (he had won the Shellsport round at Oulton the previous July),

*Brands Hatch-based Motor Circuit Developments owned Oulton Park as well as Snetterton and Mallory Park. MCD's manager, John Webb, was largely responsible for introducing F5000 in 1969, basing it on the successful American Formula A. Webb also instigated Formula Ford, and, later, its offspring, FF2000 and Sports 2000.

In the 1973 Gold Cup race, Peter Gethin slips his works-entered Chevron B24 through on the inside to take the lead as Tony Dean's similar car runs wide at Old Hall. The result was a Chevron 1-2-3, with Teddy Pilette also managing to put his Team VDS car ahead of Dean to take second place.

On a still damp but drying track, Gethin's Team VDS Lola T400 throws up the spray exiting Lodge Corner, ahead of Vern Schuppan's Lola T332 during the Gold Cup race in September 1975. Schuppan finished second, having passed Pilette's Lola T400 three laps from the end of the 50-lap race. Gethin finished fourth.

while local rising star, Kim Mather, took the F2 class. A year later the grid for the 25th Gold Cup was twice as strong, and Irishman David Kennedy took the victory in his Wolfrace-sponsored Wolf WR4 after Rupert Keegan's Arrows A1B retired with brake problems.

The last big race of the decade at Oulton, round 9 of the 1979 Aurora series in June, was won by Emilio de Villota's ex-Gunnar Nilsson Lotus 78 from Bernard de Dryver's Fittipaldi F5A, and motor cycle legend Giacomo Agostini's Williams FW06.

So, whilst the cars – and many of the drivers – may

have seen more glorious times, such was the wealth of Grand Prix history and experience throughout the field that Formula 1's 'return' to Oulton was very welcome, and Cheshire racegoers were once again able to relish the sight and sound of modern Grand Prix cars driven to the limit on one of the best circuits anywhere in the world.

Although not strictly an Oulton Park race, one other major event brought some of the greatest names in motor sport back to the Cheshire circuit in the early 1970s – the Tour of Britain. Introduced in the summer of 1973, the Tour was similar to the great RAC Rally of the time, but with circuit races as well as rally special stages held at various venues all around Great Britain. It attracted both race and rally drivers, and one of the races, naturally, was at Oulton Park. Grand Prix star and future World Champion, James Hunt, won the inaugural Tour of Britain driving Richard Lloyd's Chevrolet Camaro, ably assisted by his navigator, journalist Robert Fearnall, whose family, interestingly, had strong ties with Oulton Park. Double World Champion, Graham Hill, was also entered, at the wheel of a Datsun saloon. The following year it was the turn of the rally specialists to prevail, the great Roger Clark winning overall in his Ford Escort. Although the Tour of Britain ran for only a couple of years, it has recently been revived as Tour Britannia, a classic car event, again passing through Oulton Park on its way around the country.

What 50 laps of a dry, or nearly dry, Oulton Park can do to a 'rain' tyre. This was third-placed Pilette's rear tyre at the finish of the 1975 Gold Cup. Not a lot of life left in it.

Far left, inset: Winner of the 1975 Gold Cup was David Purley in the unique 3.4-litre, V6 Cosworth-powered Chevron B30. Purley had persuaded Derek Bennett to build the car for F5000 and base it on the B29 Formula 2 Chevron, the smaller, lighter chassis taking advantage of smaller engines now permitted in the formula alongside the 5-litre V8s.

Left, inset: 1975 was also the year, of course, that snow caused Thursday's practice for the Good Friday F5000 race to be abandoned. David Purley (left) and Australian, Dave Walker, look happy enough in the still snow-covered paddock on race morning.

Left: By the morning of the race, with much use of salt, the snow had been cleared off the tarmac and practice went ahead. This was also the first meeting at which the new, shortened circuit was used.

Most of the background snow had melted away by the time the race started. Teddy Pilette had worked his Team VDS Lola T400 into the lead when engine trouble intervened and dropped him to sixth. Here, he leads the Lola T332 of eventual winner, Gordon Spice, the long-time supporter of F5000 deservedly enjoying his first win in the category.

A year earlier on Good Friday, 1974, two British drivers – by then more often to be seen racing in America – were separated by a mere 0.2s after 30 laps of the full Oulton Park circuit. The winner was Brian Redman at the wheel of the Lola T332-Chevrolet entered by Sid Taylor, but he was so very nearly caught by David Hobbs when his rear wing began to collapse five laps from the end. The picture shows Redman at Knicker Brook on his penultimate lap. Earlier, Redman had established a new outright lap record in 1m 24.0s, a time equalled before he retired by Teddy Pilette (Chevron B28).

At the drivers' briefing before the race, Brian Redman, nearest to the camera, is flanked by entrant Sid Taylor, and, left, Teddy Pilette.

Cresting the brow which is the 'sting in the tail' of Druids Corner, Australian, Vern Schuppan, is on the way to third place on the grid for the 1974 Gold Cup race. Driving the same Sid Taylor/Teddy Yip Theodore Racing Lola T332 with which Brian Redman had been victorious on Good Friday, Schuppan was destined to be an early retirement from the following day's race after over-revving the engine in his efforts to wrest the lead from Peter Gethin and eventual winner, Ian Ashley.

Left: Although still counting toward the Shellsport European F5000 Championship, races in 1976 were officially run to Group 8 regulations. At Oulton Park, the 1976 Gold Cup was won by Guy Edwards' ex-John Watson RAM Racing Brabham BT42/44, the first F1 car to win the race for four years. Brian "Superhen" Henton's F2 Boxer PR762 was second.

Guy looks well pleased with his day's work. It's interesting to see how the shape of the Gold Cup changed over the years. Compare it with David Purley's the year before (top right), and the one proudly displayed by David Kennedy on his lap of honour in 1979.

Motor Racing at Oulton Park in the 1970s

The Gold Cup was back to a Good Friday date for 1977 and Britain's new World Champion, James Hunt, was there to drop the starting flag and present the awards.

Also making a very welcome appearance at Oulton Park for the Gold Cup was 5-times Le Mans winner, Derek Bell, who was driving a Hexagon-entered Penske PC3. It was Bell's first race at Oulton Park for nine years; his last was when he drove a Ferrari 312 in the 1968 Gold Cup alongside team-mate Chris Amon. Guy Edwards was on pole in his Ford V6-engined March, rebuilt after a crash during testing at Oulton earlier in the week, but it was Bell who took the lead when Hunt dropped the Union Jack. Into Foster's, he is chased by Australian, Bruce Allison (Chevron B37), Guy Edwards, and the rest of the 17-car field.

James Hunt and Derek Bell with the winner's laurels after the race.

Fastest of the Formula 2 cars in practice had been the Lola T462 of popular Irishman, Alo Lawler, here seen at Old Hall. On lap 11 of the Gold Cup race, the Lola suffered the most enormous accident as it crested the very fast Clay Hill, destroyed itself against the barriers and came to rest in the middle of the track, immediately halting the race. Miraculously, Lawler, who was removed to hospital, escaped serious injury and the race was restarted, giving the World Champion a second opportunity to wave the flag.

Lawler was back on the grid at Oulton for the next Shellsport race three months later. As the field heads for Old Hall Corner for the first time, Tony Trimmer leads Guy Edwards (March 751), Divina Galica (Surtees TS19), Val Musetti (March 761), Bruce Allison (Chevron B37), and the first F2 car, Norman Dickson's March.

Winner of the July race and Shellsport champion in 1977 was Tony Trimmer, who drove a Surtees TS19 entered by Melchester Racing. During the race, he equalled Guy Edwards' lap record, set in 1976.

1978's Gold Cup race was the first round of the new Aurora AFX Formula 1 Championship. Trimmer and Edwards were still leading the way, the former now McLaren M23-mounted. Trimmer leads the small field through Old Hall ahead of Emilio de Villota's similar car, Guy Edwards' March (hidden), and Teddy Pilette in the Stanley BRM P207. Geoff Lees, Alo Lawler, and Mike Wilds follow.

With championship leader Trimmer absent (he was conserving his resources for an attempt to qualify for the British GP three weeks later), Emilio de Villota (McLaren M23) leads away from the start of the Aurora AFX round in June 1978. Guy Edwards in the Titbits March 781, and Bob Evans in John Cooper's Hesketh 308C, are in pursuit. Formula 2 protagonists, Mike Wilds (Ralt RT1 number 6) and Kim Mather (Chevron B35D, number 15) are right behind Evans.

Edwards won the race from team-mate Bruce Allison, whose car he was driving following a coming together between the two in practice. Allison was forced to start from the back of the grid as he had changed to a different car (March 761). While everyone else chose slicks, the two March drivers chose wets for what turned out to be quite a wet race.

On the podium, Edwards uncorks the Moet watched by Bruce Allison, left, and Val Musetti on the right. Stepping up next to Edwards to join the fun is Teddy Pilette who brought the Stanley BRM P207 home in fourth place behind the three Marches.

Introduced in 1973, the Avon Motor Tour of Britain, organised by the BRSCC, attracted some very famous names to Oulton Park, one of the many race circuits which, along with rally-type special stages, were interspersed in the countrywide itinerary. The 100-car entry, divided into the four price classes fashionable in production saloon racing of the era, included Graham Hill at the wheel of a Datsun Bluebird, which was in the £1050-£1500 class.

James Hunt took over the Alan Rivers Chevrolet Camaro entry when its regular driver, Richard Lloyd, was injured in a road accident. With *Autosport's* Robert Fearnall as navigator, the pair surprised themselves by winning the event overall. Here, James hurls the Camaro through Old Hall ahead of Tony Lanfranchi's BMW 3.0 Si. In case you're wondering, both were in the over £1500 class ...

Above: The 1974 Tour of Britain drew the great and the good of British rallying and production saloon racing in an entry which again included James Hunt, this time driving a Vauxhall Magnum, and Jody Scheckter in a Ford Capri navigated by Eoin Young. With more special stages included in the competition, perhaps it was not surprising that the winner was rally champion, Roger Clark, here demonstrating his artistry at Lodge Corner.

Another rally man, Tony Pond, with David 'ProDrive' Richards in the navigator's seat, won the 1975 Tour which no longer visited Oulton and was the last of the series – until, that is, its reincarnation thirty years later as the Tour Britannia for historic cars.

One F5000 driver whose career was on a strong upward path was Australian, Alan Jones, here leading the 1975 Gold Cup race in the 3.4-litre March 751 entered by RAM before engine trouble caused his retirement. Five years later, he would be World Champion.

Rising stars

Whilst Formula 5000 and British F1 were the star attractions, two other single seater formulae regularly headlined some of the best Oulton Park race meetings throughout the 1970s. Formula 3 and Formula Atlantic were both considered training grounds for aspiring Grand Prix drivers, the former being an almost compulsory way-point on the route to the top.

Two decades had passed since Formula 3 had first taken up this important role, and, since 1964, the formula had been enjoying one of its classic periods, the era of the 1-litre 'screamer' engines, characterised by exciting multi-car slipstreaming contests. This epoch ended in 1971 with the introduction of new rules which raised the capacity limit to 1600cc, but strangled the engines by severely restricting the air intake to the carburettors of the production-based engines. The effect was to reduce engine speed, drastically quieten the cars and provoke argument and protest over 'leaking' air boxes which could 'accidentally' give rise to significant increases in power.

In 1974, the engine capacity limit was raised to two litres, still with restricted air intake: over thirty years later these engine regulations remain virtually unchanged for Formula 3.

Among the drivers who tasted success in F3, and who raced at Oulton Park during the 1970s en route to greater things, were Tony Brise, Alan Jones, Brian Henton, Gunnar Nilsson, Danny Sullivan, Bruno Giacomelli, Alex Ribeiro, Geoff Lees, Derek Daly, Derek Warwick, Nelson Piquet, Chico Serra, Stefan Johansson, Andrea De Cesaris, and, towards the end of the decade, Nigel Mansell.

With F3 apparently in decline and the next major

step on the ladder, Formula 2, demanding stratospheric budgets, MCD's John Webb was instrumental in importing America's Formula B to the UK under the name Formula Atlantic, its first year being 1971. As with F5000 and its transatlantic counterpart, Formula A, there were one or two minor regulations differences between the US and UK versions.

Both formulae demanded production-based engines from 1100cc to 1600cc, but, in the UK, fuel injection was not allowed. However, the Formula Atlantic regulations did allow the multi-valve heads, and the 4-valve Cosworth BDA engine, once reduced from its homologated 1601cc capacity, became the engine to have. (When Canada adopted the UK regulations for its Formula Atlantic racing in 1974, the USA rules were changed to admit the BDA.) Other requirements included a maximum of five gears, a minimum weight of 440kg, and a fuel capacity of no more than 15 gallons. Formula Atlantic was immediately popular; the cars were fast, they *sounded* like racing cars and cost far less to run than F2 – and probably even F3 – and the racing was often close and exciting. They were also faster than F3.

Having raced in Formula Ford – with a Lola T200 that was the prize for winning a racing school championship – and Formula SuperVee, and scoring a debut win in F3 at Brands Hatch the previous year, Welshman, Tom Pryce, was racing a works Royale RP12 in Formula Atlantic in 1973. But for an off-course excursion at Cascades while chasing David Purley's March for the lead in the closing laps, he so nearly won the opening round of that year's BP Championship at Oulton in March. He won the Grovewood Award in 1973, and went on to Formula 1 with the Shadow team until a terrible accident claimed his life at Kyalami, during the South African Grand Prix of 1977.

The first champion, winner of the Yellow Pages series in 1971, was Australian, Vern Schuppan, driving a works Palliser. Other stars of Formula Atlantic between 1971 and 1975 included Tony Brise, Colin Vandervell, David Purley, Jim Crawford, Gunnar Nilsson, Ted Wentz, ex-Mini racer Dave Morgan, and New Zealander, John Nicholson, who won championships in both 1973 and 1974.

Left: Another highly talented British driver to make it into Grands Prix, only to lose his life in tragic circumstances, was Dartford-born Tony Brise. A karter since the age of eight and National Champion in 1969, he moved to FF1600 in 1970. By September of 1973, Tony Brise had swapped his earlier GRD 373 for a more competitive March 733, and, in the John Player F3 Championship race which supported that year's Gold Cup event, is seen very closely following the similar car of Richard Robarts into Cascades with Alan Jones' GRD right behind. Brise went on to win that year's John Player Championship from Jones by two points, and also took the Lombard North Central title ahead of Robarts, although both had the same points total.

Following two very successful years in Formula Atlantic, mostly with the works Modus team, Brise made his GP debut in a Williams at the 1975 Spanish GP, before moving to Graham Hill's Embassy Hill team when the former World Champion retired from driving mid-season. In November, both Hill and Brise were among those who perished when Hill's light aircraft crashed during landing at Elstree, north of London, when returning from testing at the Paul Ricard circuit in France.

Before the John Player Formula Atlantic round in May 1974, Tony Brise talks to circuit commentator, Anthony Marsh, watched by a smiling Jim Crawford. Jim would go on to win the race while Tony was to finish fourth in his brand new Modus M3.

Formula Atlantic's popularity was not destined to be long-lived, however, and, by the mid-1970s, it had veered off course into something called Indylantic, whilst Formula 3 was re-establishing its position as the place to be for anyone with Grand Prix ambitions.

As F3 was – and is – to Grand Prix racing, so Formula Ford was to F3. Another John Webb creation, FF1600 featured at just about every Oulton Park race meeting, and was the principal attraction at many during the 1970s. Launched in 1967, Formula Ford had come to be regarded not only as fun racing in its own right, but also the first step on the ladder to a serious racing career. Among those taking this first step was one Nigel Mansell, who won the appropriately named Dunlop "Star of Tomorrow" race which opened the 1976 Oulton Park Gold Cup meeting.

Jim Crawford's first Formula Atlantic Championship race win had come just eight days earlier when he drove Steve Choularton's March 73B to first place in the MCD Championship race ahead of Geoff Friswell and Matt Spitzley. Here, Crawford leads Spitzley and Friswell as they approach Lodge Corner.

Eddie Jordan, best known for his Jordan Racing F1 team, also raced in Formula Atlantic, appearing in an ex-Alan Jones March in 1977, and winning the Irish Formula Atlantic Championship the following year. He went on to drive in F3 and, briefly, F2, before turning to team ownership. But in 1975 he was a leading competitor in Formula Ford 1600, here dicing in his Crossle 30F with Tiff Needell (Elden) and Derek Warwick (Hawke DL12). Eddie finished second in his heat and fourth in the final of the British Air Ferries round on this June day.

Left: The finale of the 1974 John Player Atlantic International Championship came down to a straight race between Jim Crawford and John Nicholson at Oulton Park in early October. Crawford, who had just signed a contract with Team Lotus for 1975 (unfortunate timing, as it turned out, as Lotus was at a low ebb, struggling with its once successful but now outdated Type 72), had an engine fail during practice, resulting in engine and number swapping with team-mate, Choularton, and prolonged argument between team and officials about what could and could not be changed within the rules.

Crawford's victorious rival for the 1974 John Player Atlantic Championship was New Zealander, John Nicholson, who had set up his engine tuning business in England in partnership with McLaren, supplying the F1 team with its Cosworth DFV units. Nicholson already had one Formula Atlantic Championship to his name, having won the BP Championship the previous year in his Lyncar.

There was no doubt about who the spectators wanted to win! But the coronation of the local favourite was not to happen as a sixth lap coming together with arch rival, Nicholson, as they diced for fourth place, put the March out altogether, leaving Nicholson's Lyncar damaged but able to press on and finish the 20-lap race in sixth place, enough to take the crown.

Things didn't always go to plan. In March 1975, Eddie helps the marshals move his stricken Crossle after a visit to the Old Hall barriers. The year ended on an even worse note with a late season crash in which he broke both his legs, rather ruining his plans for 1976 ...

The 1975 British Formula 3 Champion was Swede, Gunnar Nilsson. Following practice for the July round of the BP Super Visco Championship, Gunnar holds up the practice times for Modus driver, Danny Sullivan, BAF March driver, Rupert Keegan, and his fellow works March driver, Alex Ribeiro. Nilsson's luck was out in the race, his fire extinguisher spontaneously discharging itself for no apparent reason during the warm-up lap. Sullivan won the race from Richard Hawkins, whose March started from pole position. In the championship, Ribeiro finished runner-up to Nilsson, with Sullivan third.

Left: Another of the sizeable contingent of Irish drivers making a name for themselves in the 1970s was Derek Daly, here entertaining commentator, Neville Hay, in a pre-race interview before driving his Van Diemen RF76 in the Townsend Thoresen FF1600 race in March 1976. At the end of the year, he won the Formula Ford Festival in a Hawke, elevating him to F3 and another championship the following year in a Chevron. By 1978, he was in F2 and had made his GP debut.

Daly eventually moved to the USA, racing in CART and Indycar as well as sports cars, retiring from driving in 1992 and taking up the microphone as a commentator with the ESPN TV sports channel.

Gunnar Nilsson, seen during practice for the March 1975 F3 round at Oulton Park, joined Team Lotus the following year, partnering 1978 World Champion, Mario Andretti, and winning the Belgian Grand Prix in 1977. Sadly, later that year, he was diagnosed with cancer. His great compatriot, Ronnie Peterson, then raced alongside Andretti in what turned out to be one of Lotus' most successful seasons. It was only a few weeks after Peterson's tragic death following the Monza accident that Gunnar Nilsson passed away.

In 1973, six years after he first came to Britain to race and seven years before he became World Champion, Australian, Alan Jones, began to achieve the results he had always wanted. Driving a GRD 373, he finished a close second to Tony Brise in that year's John Player Formula 3 International Championship. At Oulton Park in April for the second round, which had 54 entries, no less, Alan won his heat from pole position and finished second in the final. Following him home in the heat but crashing out of the final was Larry Perkins in his year-old GRD. Here, the two Australians line up for the fast left-hander, Island Bend, with the Dunlop Bridge at Clay Hill visible in the distance.

Spot the difference! In 1978, there was almost nothing to choose between Britain's Derek Warwick and Brazilian, Nelson Piquet. Both driving Ralt RT1s, the pair dominated the two British F3 championships, Piquet winning the BP Super Visco title ahead of Warwick, their positions reversed in the Vandervell series. Chico Serra finished equal second with Warwick on points in the BP Championship and took third place in the Vandervell standings.

Piquet's first F1 race also came in 1978, driving an Ensign in the German GP. In 1979 he joined the Brabham F1 team and, after finishing runner-up to Alan Jones in 1980, went on to win the World Championship three times, in 1981, 1983, and 1987.

Right: In 1977, future World Champion, Nigel Mansell, had been making his presence felt in Formula Ford 1600, first in the Javelin JL5 seen here in May, and, later in the year, at the wheel of his Crossle 32F. The previous year, at the Oulton Park Gold Cup meeting, he had convincingly won his heat and the final of the Dunlop Star of Tomorrow FF race in a two-year-old Hawke DL11.

Close racing: first corner action in the BP F3 round in April 1978. Chico Serra (March 783) leads the field through Old Hall, with Piquet and Warwick side-by-side, and Nigel Mansell's plain white March 783 just visible behind Warwick. Next up is Philip Bullman (Chevron B38) who was to work his way into the lead only to be disqualified for a yellow flag infringement, leaving the race win to Serra. Mansell's race, unfortunately, ended against the Knicker Brook barriers on the first lap.

In only his sixth race, and with his novice's cross still on the back of his Toyota Celica, 17-year-old Martin Brundle was on pole
for the up-to-1600cc race in the Tricentrol British Saloon Car Championship round which supported the 1976 Gold Cup race.
He was leading the race from Bernard Unett's Chrysler Avenger, and Richard Lloyd's VW Golf Gti, when a punctured rear tyre
caused him to spin into retirement at Cascades on the fourth lap.

... and one for all

Saloon car racing has been popular with the spectating public since its introduction in the 1950s, when the competing cars really were – or could have been – straight out of the showroom. The reason usually put forward for this popularity was that the 'man in the street' could see 'his' car performing on-track. Throughout the sixties, it was Mini versus Jaguar, Lotus Cortina versus Ford Galaxie, and so on, but, gradually, development and modification took the racing variant ever further from the 'showroom' version until a completely separate species, the Special Saloon, was defined. Some of these cars, in truth, were simply single seater racing cars, clothed in a fibreglass body of similar proportions to those of some carefully chosen production vehicle. As engine location, ie front or rear, had to remain unchanged, cars such as the rear-engined Skoda became popular in this class of racing.

Nothing wrong with any of that, of course, and some

It's March 1974, the last year of the full circuit unfettered by chicanes, and the Motorcraft Escort Mexico Challenge field heads full tilt down the straight from Hill Top into the right-hander at Knicker Brook, Colin Vandervell leading from the Thomas Motors car of Neil McGrath, who later reigned supreme in Renault 5 racing.

For the following year, *Penthouse* magazine assumed the sponsorship role of what was now the Ford Escort Championship, the newly introduced Escort Sport 1600 admitted to the series alongside the Mexicos. John Morris leads a group through Old Hall, with Mike Freeman taking a short cut across the grass.

The tyre-squealing, body-rolling Renault 5s had their own series in 1974, sponsored by Renault Ltd. At this round of the Renault 5 Challenge, held at the July meeting which also hosted the Avon Tour of Britain, Mick Hill, in number 19, demonstrates some of the finer points of Renault 5 driving as he pursues Dave Hodges out of Old Hall Corner.

Left: The ubiquitous Mini was not to be outdone by the French cars, and appeared in various guises; these are two of the 'big boys,' the 1275GTs, scrapping over second place in the Leyland Cars National Mini 1275 Championship race at the BBC Radio 1 meeting in May 1976. Touring car star to be, Steve Soper, successfully resisted all of series leader, Alan Curnow's desperate attempts to get past and held on to his place, finishing behind winner Paul Taft.

truly impressive creations took to the tracks in the 1970s: fast and great fun to watch and, no doubt, to drive. Against this background production saloon car racing was also growing in popularity, not only with competitors and spectators but, crucially, with manufacturers, who well appreciated the publicity potential of racing success.

But how to guarantee that success? Simple: banish any other make or model from the competition! The 1970s saw a plethora of one-make race series laid before the motor racing public, with umpteen different classes of Minis, Ford Escorts and Fiestas, Renault 5s, Sunbeams, and, eventually, even BMW getting in on the act. For the manufacturer concerned it was a guaranteed

win whatever happened, and for the spectator, it has to be said, the racing was usually close and frequently spectacular to watch.

The Ford Motor Company was an early advocate. Hannu Mikkola and Gunnar Palm had won the 1970 London to Mexico World Cup Rally in an 1850cc Ford Escort GT, and the company launched the 'Escort Mexico' to capitalise on this success. With its strengthened 2-door bodyshell and RS brakes and suspension – not to mention contrasting colour body stripe or modest 86bhp – the model was ideal for sporting use. The Motorcraft Mexico Challenge provided the opportunity; the sponsor, Motorcraft, being Ford's own spare parts division.

Many other one-make series were to ensue in the UK and elsewhere. What follows, in the space available, is a taste of some of the more popular series of the 1970s.

Full grids and close racing were also features of the Leyland Mini 7 Challenge. Here, the field cascades down into Foster's on the opening lap of the championship round at Oulton in October 1976.

A rather strange variation on the one-make theme was the BMW County Championship, in which various drivers were invited by BMW to race one of twelve of its 323i models, all prepared by TWR. Each car represented an English county – and a BMW dealer from that county. For some reason, Cheshire was not among the favoured shires ... The races all supported Aurora AFX British F1 rounds, and, in this one in June 1979, John Bright leads the field through Old Hall on behalf of Lancashire. But it was Tony Dron who won from Win Percy and Tiff Needell; or, if you prefer, Nottingham, Avon and Hertfordshire.

And, finally, to close this chapter, Mexicos in the sunset! This was my attempt to summarise that slightly melancholy end-of-season feeling when the year's racing is about to end, and months of cold, dark days separate us from the next race meeting. As the sun goes down, a train of Escort Mexicos heads down the Avenue at the last meeting of 1973, Rod Mansfield leading the way. With the 'energy crisis' about to bring the prospect of petrol rationing, the winter of 1973-74 was a particularly bleak one ...

Those ARE the days!

Every year, since 1956, the Vintage Sports Car Club (VSCC) had been making a welcome visit to Oulton Park to hold a race meeting in its own inimitable style. The annual Richard Seaman Memorial Trophies meeting was unlike any other at the Cheshire circuit throughout the season; no Formula Fords, no Special Saloons, just a dazzling array of pre-1940 cars of all types. Some came to be judged in the Concours d'Elegance but most were there to compete against each other in a series of handicap and scratch races, pretty much as they had at Brooklands before WWII.

My impression, attending and photographing these meetings, was – and still is – that they were not an attempt to relive the past – let alone try to recreate it – but that, for all involved, it was simply a continuation of racing as it had always been, which simply revolved

cnt'd page 59

Left: Big cars and big personalities are part of the attraction of a vintage race meeting. This is the Barnato Hassan Bentley, built in the 1930s for racing at Brooklands, where it lapped at over 143mph. Originally with an engine of "only" 6½ litres, this was soon increased to 8 litres. At the wheel is Keith Schellenberg, whose colourful career included being a member of the 1956 Olympic bobsleigh team, captaining the Yorkshire county rugby team, and being owner and Laird of the Hebridean island of Eigg. On this occasion in 1975, the first time the vintage meeting had been held on the short Foster's circuit, the pairing finished second in the Seaman Vintage Trophy race to Bernard Kain's more nimble Bugatti.

Another crowd-pleasing giant, once described as 'The Ultimate Laxative,' is the Bentley Napier, but this one was built as late as 1968 by Peter Morley, here seen depositing tyre rubber at Lodge Corner. With a chassis originally from an 8-litre Bentley, the car is powered by a 24-litre Napier Lion aero engine, its three banks of four cylinders arranged in W-formation. The car has since passed to Chris Williams, who continues to delight the spectators by turning rubber into smoke and noise at VSCC events.

Motor Racing at Oulton Park in the 1970s

Left: Variety is indeed one of the key attractions of vintage racing, as illustrated by this group of cars rounding the banked Esso Bend (later renamed Shell), with the lake in the background, during the 1974 Seaman Historic Trophy race. Geoffrey St John's twin-ohc, supercharged Bugatti Type 51 leads Jonathan Abson's Lagonda, Colin Warrington's Appleton Spl (number 43), Keith Knight in his Riley Special, R Masters' MG (45), and David Fletcher-Jones' Lagonda.

Resourcefulness is another key attribute of the vintage racer. At the 1977 Seaman meeting, Keith Knight's Riley Special, seen in the previous picture, suffered camshaft problems during practice. The quickest way to replace the camshaft would have been with the engine lying on its side (to avoid losing cam followers, etc), but, with insufficient time to remove the engine, there was only one thing to do: turn the whole car onto its side! Work is well under way, supervised by the car's builder and driver who leans over, resting his arm on the car's front wheel, and was completed in time for him to join everyone on the grid for the Historic Trophy race.

A post-war car, Bill Wilks' Cooper Bristol won the Seaman Historic Trophy in 1956, but, thereafter, the rule which restricted the race to pre-1940 cars was quickly reinstated. An allcomers scratch event became a regular feature of VSCC races, allowing front-engined, single seater racing cars built before 1961 to show their paces alongside some of the vintage and historic cars seen in other races. This is Scotsman, Ray Fielding, taking Old Hall in his recently-acquired Maserati A6GCM, forerunner of the 250F, at the 1973 Seaman meeting.

A sense of humour and an even greater sense of history are apparent in this little notice spotted on the wheel of an Alfa Romeo in the Oulton Park paddock in 1977. It was there, we can be sure, not as a boast but simply as a sobering reminder of the hallowed footsteps in which the driver was following. My records do not indicate which car bore the message, but it was quite possibly this Alfa Romeo P3, recently returned from Argentina and driven in crowd-pleasing fashion by Alain de Cadenet in the Seaman Historic race.

around the cars known and loved by their owners and drivers. While the list of drivers may have changed year upon year, often with succeeding generations of the same family taking over, the cars remained largely the same; quite the opposite of most contemporary racing. As such, it is not so much a case of "those were the days" as one of "those still *are* the days."

The two big races at these meetings were for 'vintage,' ie pre-1931, and 'historic' racing cars which,

in VSCC terms, is to say that they were built before 1940. The winners of each race on scratch (there was also a concurrent handicap) received a trophy named in memory of Richard Seaman, the great British Grand Prix driver of the 1930s who, as a member of the mighty Mercedes-Benz team, memorably won the German Grand Prix in 1938. He died the following year after crashing at Spa.

Although the VSCC is all about pre-war cars, its

Footnote: Subsequently, after an absence of seven years, the VSCC returned to Oulton Park in 2005. The feature races at its June meeting are now named after Mike Hawthorn, Britain's first World Champion, the Seaman Trophy races having been transferred to another of the Club's major events at Donington Park.

Those ARE the days!

ERAs have been dominant in the Seaman Historic races since G R Hartwell won the first one at Silverstone in 1950. English Racing Automobiles was founded in the 1930s by Humphrey Cook, Raymond Mays and Peter Berthon, and was, in effect, the forerunner of post-war British Racing Motors or BRM. Although the concern made only 17 ERAs, sixteen of them have survived, and most of these are still racing. They are still individually identified by their chassis numbers.

The Honourable Patrick Lindsay drove one of the most famous of these charismatic cars, chassis number R5B, but perhaps better known as 'Remus,' the name it was originally given when it was raced by Siamese driver B Bira as part of his White Mouse Stable. Lindsay's Seaman Trophy wins began with a hat trick in 1961-1963; he won again in 1965 and yet again in 1979.

programme did include an 'allcomers' race which catered for pre-1961, front-engined racing cars such as Maserati 250Fs, Connaughts and Cooper-Bristols – but not for sports cars.

This was a matter of particular concern to the renowned motor sport photographer, Guy Griffiths, who lamented the lack of opportunity for owners of great cars of the 1950s, such as the Jaguar C- and D-Types and Aston Martin DB3S, to use their cars in competition. Too many such cars were in danger of being inappropriately modified in an effort to make them competitive with more modern machinery, exported to America – or both.

The Porsche Club of Great Britain and the Frazer Nash Car Club stepped in and put on a race at their jointly promoted Snetterton meeting in 1966 for what were called 'Griffiths Formula' sports-racing cars; ie, those built between 1940 and 1955. In many ways, this was the start of the interest in 'historic'

cnt'd page 65

Even more successful in the Seaman Historic Trophy was Martin Morris, who, by the end of the 1970s, had scored seven victories, five of them in succession from 1973 to 1977. To add to that, in 1973 he won *both* the Vintage and the Historic Seaman Trophies, borrowing Hamish Morton's 3/4½-litre Bentley, seen here opposite locking out of Lodge, to take victory in the Vintage event.

In 1974, Morris won the Seaman Historic race. Sir John Venables-Llewelyn in R4A, the ex-Pat Fairfield and later Bob Gerard car, had been scrapping with Patrick Marsh, who was at the wheel of the 1½-litre ERA once driven by Richard Seaman. Then R4A's engine began overheating and, to avoid serious damage, the car was retired out on the circuit. Having collected his winner's laurels, Martin Morris also experienced engine problems on his lap of honour, and stopped to share a tow home with Venables-Llewelyn.

For the fifth year in succession, Martin Morris receives the Seaman Historic Trophy winner's laurels in 1977. Morris, who was production director of the Devon dairy foods company best known for its Ambrosia product range, drove the 2-litre R11B first raced by Reggie Tongue, and later – mainly in hillclimbs and sprints – by Ken Wharton. His car not having been blessed with a classical moniker like some of its rivals, Morris named it 'Humphrey.'

Turning to more modern machinery, Martin Morris was equally at home at the wheel of his D-Type Jaguar, OKV 3, here being pursued down The Avenue by Frank Sytner in a Maserati 'Birdcage' Tipo 61 during the JCB/Speed Merchants historic car race in April 1975. As a Jaguar works car, OKV 3 won at Reims in 1954, and, in the hands of Mike Hawthorn, broke the lap record at Silverstone.

Above: As an example of the high quality fields which the JCB/Speed Merchants series was able to bring together in the mid-1970s, the race which supported the 1974 Gold Cup would take some beating. As the race gets under way, eventual winner, Neil Corner, in the centre of the front row, smokes his BRM's tyres, while Willie Green in Anthony Bamford's Lister Chevrolet on pole, and John Harper's Lister Jaguar nose ahead. Just above the right headlight of Harper's car – yes, it's Martin Morris again, in his faithful ERA sitting head and shoulders above the rest of the field.

A few rows further back and with light rain falling, Richard Bond waits patiently in Robert Cooper's Cooper-Bristol. His reward was to take second place in the 2-litre class. Bond was another very experienced driver who excelled in historic racing, particularly in his Lola T70 and, before that, one of the original HWM-Jaguars, registered HWM 1.

Left: As the grid assembles for that 1974 race, Tom Wheatcroft (right, in black and yellow Dunlop jacket), owner of Donington Park circuit and the racing car collection whose BRM P25 Neil Corner was about to drive to victory, seems to be glancing anxiously in the direction of Willie Green's Lister Chevrolet, which had 'stolen' pole position when Corner missed part of qualifying.

racing which really began to take off during the 1970s. Hard to believe now but, at the time, it was seen as a low-cost route to going motor racing as the cars were cheap compared with new, contemporary racing cars.

The Historic Sports Car Club (HSCC) came into being in 1969 and promoted racing for historic sports cars and single seaters, although it would be another ten years before it organised its own first race meeting. An extremely important influence in establishing historic sports car racing in the early 1970s, however, was the Liverpool-based organisation, Speed Merchants. The founder of Speed Merchants was Nigel Moores, a member of the Littlewoods football pools family and owner of a superb collection of historic cars, most of

cnt'd page 70

Left: After ten action-packed laps dicing with Corner's BRM, dropping back only when the engine temperature rose to worrying levels, Willie Green acknowledges the applause that greeted his first in class and second place overall.

It could *almost* be a scene from the 1950s, but actually is the same September 1974 meeting when Alain de Cadenet was racing his newly-acquired Ferrari 625 Grand Prix car for the first time. The car, which had been imported from America by Anthony Bamford, needed some persuasion to get started, but, once it did, went on to finish the race second in class.

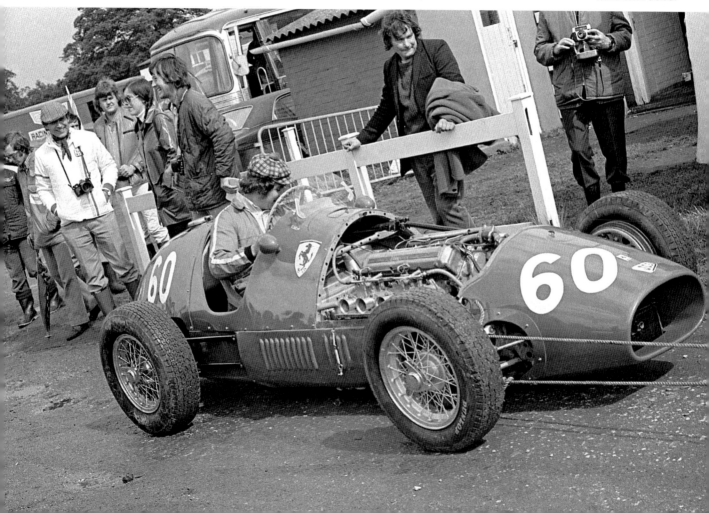

Undoubtedly, one of the major appeals of historic car racing for the spectator is being able to see the drivers at work. This is Peter van Rossem ably demonstrating his art at the wheel of his Cooper-Bristol as it powers its way out of Foster's in 1975.

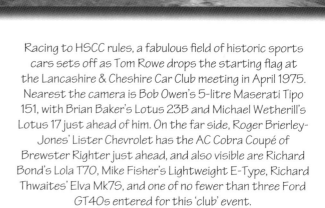

Right: Paul Weldon's first drive in his newly-acquired 5-litre, Gulf-liveried GT40 Mirage came in a very, very wet post-Historic Sports Car race at the L&CCC August meeting in 1974. At least practice had been on a dry track, and he drove well to bring the car, which had raced at Le Mans in 1967 but spent most of its racing career in southern Africa, home in second place overall.

Racing to HSCC rules, a fabulous field of historic sports cars sets off as Tom Rowe drops the starting flag at the Lancashire & Cheshire Car Club meeting in April 1975. Nearest the camera is Bob Owen's 5-litre Maserati Tipo 151, with Brian Baker's Lotus 23B and Michael Wetherill's Lotus 17 just ahead of him. On the far side, Roger Brierley-Jones' Lister Chevrolet has the AC Cobra Coupé of Brewster Righter just ahead, and also visible are Richard Bond's Lola T70, Mike Fisher's Lightweight E-Type, Richard Thwaites' Elva Mk7S, and one of no fewer than three Ford GT40s entered for this 'club' event.

63 EMU, an Aston Martin works team cars of the 1950s, must be one of the most famous historic sports racers, and just the sort of car for which the historic sports car class was created. Looking absolutely immaculate in the hands of Robert Cooper, the DB3S is pictured as it exits Lodge Corner during the JCB Historic Car Championship race at the 1973 Gold Cup meeting in September of that year.

which he raced under the pseudonyms Paul Kelly or, more colourfully, Willie Eckerslyke.

Moores, with his partner, D-Type Jaguar driver, Bill Allen, set up the JCB/Speed Merchants Historic Car Championship with sponsorship from the building plant manufacturer, JCB, through the auspices of one of its directors, Anthony Bamford, another avid collector of historic racing cars.

A feature of the championship was that it brought together pre-61 sports cars, running under HSCC rules, and single seaters of the same era which were separately governed by the rules of the VSCC, a mix of closed- and open-wheeled cars which we are not likely to see today. In its first year, the JCB/Speed Merchants Championship was won jointly by Bob Owen in his 2-litre sports Maserati, and Bill Wilks with his Lotus 16 single seater.

Willie Green was the 1972 Champion, driving Anthony Bamford's 250F Maserati. It wasn't until 1973, however, when all the races were run at International meetings, that the series first came to Oulton Park, supporting that year's Gold Cup race. At about this time, major historic race meetings were becoming established at Germany's Nürburgring (the Oldtimer Grand Prix), and at other European circuits, while Britain was not to have a truly international historic event until the end of the decade.

The Lancashire and Cheshire Car Club (L&CCC) also did much to promote historic racing at Oulton Park, its regular August meeting, which featured a mixed programme of 'ancient and modern,' giving spectators another opportunity to see some fabulous cars in action again.

The field gathers in the old paddock assembly area before practice for the *Daily Mail* Speed Merchants/JCB Historic Car race at the 1975 Gold Cup meeting. Standing behind Martin Morris' D-Type Jaguar is Chris Stewart, whose HWM-Jaguar (number 3) can be seen behind car number 29, Roger Friend's Lotus 11. On the extreme right of the picture in Lister number 9 is ex-Grand Prix driver, Bruce Halford, and beyond him, Kirk Rylands looks across from his HWM Jaguar. Car 21 is the Cooper-Bristol of Robert Cooper, while just nosing in at the left is Willie Green's Maserati 250F, which was to win the race ahead of Halford and Morris.

Images of Oulton

Compiling this book has given me a lot of pleasure, revisiting photographs taken three decades and more ago. Memories have been rekindled of the cars, events, and, especially, the people, which, together, made motor racing at Oulton Park in the 1970s what it was – an exciting and enjoyable period in the sport in which it was a privilege to be involved, if only – literally – from the sidelines.

The hardest part, of course, has not been selecting which photographs to include, but – with so many to choose from – deciding which to omit. I have singled out historic racing and one-make races for attention because they are now such a prominent part of motor sport, and their origins can be traced back to the seventies. But, as the distinction between 'club' and 'national' motor racing became ever more blurred, there were many more

One of John Webb's ideas which didn't catch on was the 1975 Shellsport 4000 race, which pitted some of the more spectacular Special Saloons of the time, dubbed Superloons by some, directly against the fastest Production Saloons. To make it more equitable, the former had to make a two minute pit stop during the 50-lap final, while the production cars could run through non-stop. Two 30-lap heats sorted out who would start where for the final.

As it turned out, the grid was quite well mixed. Martin Birrane's 5-litre Capri Boss V8 and Gerry Marshall's 2.6-litre Vauxhall Firenza get away from the front row ahead of the Group 1 production Camaros of Stuart Graham, Jon Fletcher, and Andy Rouse, with Tony Sugden's Escort Special Saloon next up. With £10 going to the leader on each lap, Birrane stayed out as long as he could, and even kept his lead after his pit stop, going on to win from Marshall and Graham.

In the same Shellsport 4000 race, Alan Minshaw in his 4.8-litre, Oldsmobile-engined DAF glances towards the paddock as he powers out of Old Hall, perhaps keeping a proprietorial eye on his Demon Tweeks shop there.

categories to be enjoyed by competitor and spectator alike.

Another growing trend was the move from individual, stand-alone races toward championship series. We had Formula Ford at virtually every meeting, and such was its popularity that two, sometimes three, qualifying heats would be required to determine the field for the points-bearing final, usually with a consolation race at the end of the day's programme for the unlucky non-qualifiers. Before long, we had variations on the theme with Formula Ford 2000, and Sports 2000. For single seaters, we had Formulae Vee and Super

Vee, Formula 4 and Monopostos, while sports cars were divided into ModSports and ProdSports, each in various capacity, Clubman's, and the low-cost F750 and F1300 (née 1172) classes. Then there were the saloons, similarly split into Production and Special varieties and forming a staple part of any race programme, then as now.

What follows is a random – well, personal – selection of photographs which I hope will bring back memories for those who were lucky enough to be present at Oulton Park in the 1970s, and for those less fortunate, at least give a flavour of that era.

By 1978, Oulton Park's 25th anniversary, Derek Walker, from nearby Hale in Cheshire, was the circuit's most successful driver with 37 wins to his credit, and many more still to come. His first Ladybirds were built for the 1172 Formula and then for the Clubman's class, before he turned his attention to Formula Ford and then back to Clubmans. Ladybird Mark 10 was the last Clubman's car and had the same 1-litre Holbay power as its Fiat 850 successor, the first Ladybird Special Saloon. Here, in July 1973, Derek glances anxiously in the mirror leaving Old Hall but needn't have worried, there's no-one in sight!

Another Special Saloon built in the likeness of an improbable racer was Derek Walker's Fiat 850, actually a fully space-framed single seater powered by a 1-litre Holbay engine. The Fiat was the eleventh in Derek's very successful series of self-built cars, all named Ladybird. In torrential rain on May Day 1976, the Fiat splashes through Druids ahead of two Minis and race winner Jeff Ward's Chrysler Imp.

Peter Cartlidge's 1-litre Austin A40 was locally built, and enjoyed many successes at Oulton Park and elsewhere. Peter is seen at Old Hall during the Special Saloon Car race at the July 1975 Formula 3 meeting. The entry list for this race was full to overflowing, an indication of the popularity of the class, and Peter was initially listed as a reserve. The A40 continued its successful career for several seasons, Manchester DJ Peter Jurgens taking over the driving seat from Cartlidge.

Right: Sadly, for a circuit that, in earlier years, had hosted the RAC Tourist Trophy, there were almost no top class sports car races at Oulton Park during the 1970s. One welcome exception came in May 1976 when a round of the RAC 2-Litre Sports Car Championship was run over 25 laps. Iain McLaren's Chevron B26, here leading John Turner's Chevron B31 past the pits, was the winner. Former Chevron stalwart, John Lepp, who was leading the series, had to retire his Ultramar-backed March 76S, but not before he had set a new class lap record of 59.2 seconds.

Left: Vin Malkie began his long association with Chevrons working at Derek Bennett Engineering Ltd in Bolton where the cars were built. Now a leading preparation expert for the Chevron marque, he has for many years owned one of the very first two Chevrons built. Driving the B1 in the Shellsport Clubman's Championship race which preceded the 1973 Gold Cup, Malkie suffered this embarrassing but harmless spin at Lodge. Martin Young takes a wide line of avoidance in his Mallock U2 Mk XIB.

Ten years on, Vin had his day as winner of the Gold Cup itself, co-driving a Chevron B19 with Richard Budge. Before that, however, he put in some practice with the champagne corks (above) when he won the Historic Sports Car race at Oulton Park in May 1978.

Above: Rex Foster was one of the men responsible for introducing motor racing to Oulton Park, and, for its first 25 years, was Managing Director of Cheshire Car Circuits Ltd before handing over to Tim Parnell in 1978. Here, in April 1974, he presents the BP Man of the Meeting award to Stephen South, who had earlier dominated the Formula Ford race. South's very promising career was cut short by an accident in 1980 when he was driving a CanAm Lola for Paul Newman.

The Northern Correspondent of *Autosport*, and the magazine's regular race reporter at Oulton Park until the mid-70s, was Ian Titchmarsh (with clipboard), here, talking to Jim Crawford. The occasion was the October 1974 Formula Atlantic Championship 'showdown' between Crawford and John Nicholson when Jim's engine had failed in practice. Amid arguments with officials about whether cars could be changed between practice and race, Steve Choularton's SDC Racing team took over the scrutineering bay to get on with the work of changing engines away from the rain. To Ian's left, with the bobble hat, stands *MN* reporter and author of the definitive book on Chevron, David Gordon.

The Man with the Megaphone at the drivers' briefing, he who must be obeyed, is Clerk of the Course, John Ellison. John, who was Chairman of both the Mid-Cheshire MRC and the NW Centre of the BRSCC, was in charge for both clubs' race meetings. Demonstrating the crossed flags is Chief Observer E C Hubert, and, to his right, beyond entrant, Sid Taylor, is another of Oulton Park's regular Clerks of the Course, Tom Rowe. At the back, looking a little sceptical, perhaps, is Peter Wilshire.

While most marshals vary their post from meeting to meeting, happy to have a different view and track sector to manage, for many years, Lodge Corner was the preserve of one man, Ken Brocklehurst. Here, Ken keeps watch on 'his patch' as the 1974 Tour of Britain competitors visit the circuit for their races. Car 92 is the Moskvich 412 of Peter Jopp, and following him is John Bright in his Ford Escort. The Moskvich became popular in production saloon car racing when the classes were based on the retail price of the cars, and the cheap Russian vehicles offered the best performance to price ratio.

With big fields and close racing, Formula Ford was popular with competitor and spectator alike. This is a non-championship race with the field heading through Old Hall on the first of ten laps in March 1973.

Sometimes the racing could be too close. In March 1978, as the final of the Townsend Thoresen FF1600 round gets under way, Marc Smith's Royale flies through the air, while Mark Rogers finds himself facing the oncoming Hawke of Graham Tilley and the rest of the following pack. Thankfully, as was usually the case in such incidents, only cars and pride were damaged.

Old Hall could catch out the saloons just as easily, especially when it began to rain, as demonstrated here by the Capri of Gordon Bruce in May 1976.

Tony Dron demonstrates the 'foot hard on the throttle – opposite lock' recovery technique in his Triumph Dolomite at the Tricentrol British Saloon Car Championship round in October 1978.

Lodge Corner could be just as tricky as Old Hall. In his first season of car racing after a successful motor cycling career – in which he followed in the footsteps of his father, Les, who was the 1949 500cc World Champion – Stuart Graham manages to keep his Capri pointing in the right direction, while Les Leston spins his Camaro and Brian Cutting rotates his Capri in sympathy. Later, after borrowing Leston's car for a race at Oulton, Stuart, who lived at nearby Nantwich, bought his own Camaro and went on to win eight races with it that season, finishing third in the Castrol Championship.

When everything is going to plan, however, Old Hall can be an excellent passing place. In the National Touring Car Championship race in September 1975, the hectic dice between the Triumph Dolomites of Andy Rouse and Brian Muir, here slipping through on the inside line, resulted in a narrow class win for the UK-resident Australian driver.

Mention 1975 and thoughts immediately turn to the Easter snow storm which prevented practice for the big F5000 meeting. In the paddock, the Penthouse Racing Alfa Romeo GT Juniors of Stan Clark and Tony Dron lie abandoned under their blanket of snow. In the background, at the entrance to the paddock, are the shops, Demon Tweeks race accessories, and Chater & Scott's bookshop.

Weather can always be a factor in British motor racing, and, whilst drivers either love it or hate it, rain can sometimes benefit the photographer. Their spray lit up by the autumn sunshine, the three Chevrolet Camaros of John Brindley, Malcolm West, and Brian Pepper dive down from Lodge Corner and into Deer Leap during the Britax Production Saloon Car race in October 1974.

Meanwhile, back in the assembly area, the field for the John Player Formula Atlantic Championship race is plugging its way through the mud to get onto the circuit. Tony Brise's Modus is on wets while, behind him, Alan Jones' March is shod for dry weather. Further back, championship protagonists, John Nicholson (just behind Jones) and Jim Crawford (being directed into place by the marshal), are also on wets but would change to slicks on the grid.

Jones went on to an easy race win, even though the rain returned with two laps to go. Pole man, Brise, didn't even make it to the grid, having slid off on the newly-resurfaced Clay Hill section during his second warm-up lap.

And, finally ... the Demon Tweeks-Manchester Liners girls who memorably performed their own brand of Maori haka around Alan Minshaw's vehicle as the saloon car grid assembled. Such was the girls' devotion to their employer's interest, they even displayed his company name where it would be most admired. Those were the days!

LUBRICATION ENGINEERS
racing with
4
MANITOU
Shell
tweeks
G
R
V
LOVES For OPEL
CHESTER
46955
MANCHESTE

Also from Veloce Publishing –

ISBN 9781903706497 • £12.99*

ISBN 9781903706817 • £9.99*

ISBN 9781903706015 • £9.99*

ISBN 9781903706794 • £9.99*

ISBN 9781903706886 • £12.99*

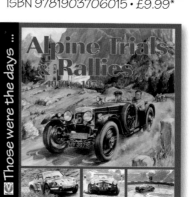

ISBN 9781904788959 • £12.99*

ISBN 9781903706862 • £9.99*

ISBN 9781904788065 • £12.99*

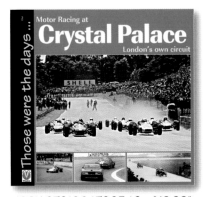

ISBN 9781904788348 • £12.99*

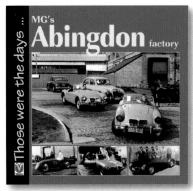

ISBN 9781845841140 • £12.99*

ISBN 9781904788669 • £12.99*

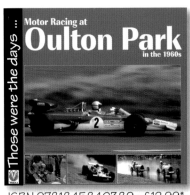

ISBN 9781845840389 • £12.99*

ISBN 9781845841645 • £12.99*

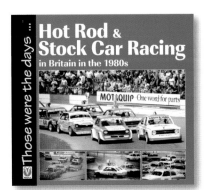

ISBN 9781845841676 • £12.99*

– with more to come!

prices subject to change. p&p extra; please call 01305 260068/visit www.veloce.co.uk for details

ISBN 9781904788317•£35.99*

Autodrome
The lost race circuits of Europe
S.S. Collins & Gavin D. Ireland

AVUS Brooklands Crystal Palace
Kristiania Maisy-kring Montlhéry Monza Nürburgring Riems Sitges

ISBN 9781845840167•£39.99*

1½-litre Grand Prix Racing 1961-65
– Low Power, High Tech

Mark Whitelock

ISBN 9781904788157•£29.99*

1950s Motorsport in colour

Martyn Wainwright

ISBN 9781904788102•£39.99*

MOTOR RACING
Reflections of a lost era
Anthony Carter

Foreword by A. David Owen, OBE

*prices subject to change. p&p extra; please call 01305
260068/visit www.veloce.co.uk for details

94

Index